The Little Book

of

Courageous Living

by

Miki Kashtan

Fearless Heart Publications

PUBLISHED

by

FEARLESS HEART PUBLICATIONS

55 Santa Clara Avenue, Suite 203,
Oakland, CA 94610
www.thefearlessheart.org

ISBN-10: 0990007316   Paperback
ISBN-13: 978-0-9900073-1-9 Paperback

For my sisters, who are my companions
every step of the way

Acknowledge

ACKNOWLEDGMENTS

This book has been a collaborative effort from the start. Lynda Smith, colleague, friend, and supporter, came up with the concept and the structure. Dozens of people provided their written notes and sent their favorite quotes. Mili Raj volunteered untold hours to create original art to illustrate this book, including layout and cover design. Perry Garfinkel collected most of the quotes that introduce the sections of this book. Dave Belden provided his keen eye and his technical expertise with CreateSpace.
This book would not be in your hands at this moment without their generous support.

TABLE OF CONTENTS

Contents

INTRODUCTION

Can you imagine truly living without a right way or a wrong way to do things? Nonviolent Communication (NVC), the path I have followed and taught since 1994, is an invitation to do just that. This little book is a collection of thoughts and ideas I have shared at workshops, talks, or in my blog, The Fearless Heart. Separately, each can serve as a focus of attention and meditation. Collectively, I put them together as a guidebook charting the course along the path of nonviolence as I aim to practice it: bringing love, courage, and a deep commitment to truth to everything we do. They are simple, evocative insights that have already touched many with whom I've shared them, providing inspiration, relief, and clarity. In fact, this compilation contains many lines sent to me by people who have attended my trainings and recorded quotes that have been particularly helpful to them in finding their own path.

Intro

These thoughts are arranged in categories that capture resonant recurring themes along with some core human values we all share. Here you will find no specific language to follow, no particular rules – only an invitation to apply yourself wholeheartedly to listening to what most matters to you and others and to aim to make life work for everyone. In so doing, I hope and trust you will find support here in these messages as you walk toward your deepest longings.

- Miki Kashtan

Authenticity

This above all:
To thine own self be true,
And it must follow, as the
night the day, Thou canst
not then be false to any
man.

– Shakespeare

Some of us have paid the price of hiding our authenticity to belong. Others have paid the price of belonging to preserve our authenticity.

I want to show up in the tremendous
imperfection of my life – my life as it is,
not my life as I wish it were.

Authenticity

I want to tell you the truth, and I want your
companionship in the truth.

Without full integration of a consciousness of nonviolence, using specific words we learn creates a gap that can show up as lack of authenticity.

Authenticity

I want to learn more and more how to express
myself in ways that are completely authentic
and require the least amount of effort for
another person to hear me.

Authentic expression and compassionate
presence are the two building blocks of
connection.

Any truth can be combined with sufficient care to maintain connection while delivering it to someone. Even a painful truth can support connection. For as long as acceptance depends on hiding the truth about who we are, it remains suspect, temporary, elusive.

Authenticity

If your only choice is between being inauthentic or using a judgment that is authentic, I would rather you use the judgment. However, I believe that a more caring and fully authentic option will almost always be available to you if you seek it.

Children

If we are to reach real peace in this world and if we are to carry on a real war against war, we shall have to begin with children; and if they will grow up in their natural innocence, we won't have to struggle; we won't have to pass fruitless idle resolutions, but we shall go from love to love and peace to peace, until at last all the corners of the world are covered with that peace and love for which consciously or unconsciously the whole world is hungering.

– Mahatma Gandhi

Showing care and interest in children's needs and presenting clearly what parents need are the breeding ground of empathic and courageous human beings who can make choices based on their deepest understanding of their own and others' needs.

We can make the lives of our children better if
we understand our choices better and if we
increase their capacity to cultivate choice
and inner freedom.

Children

The antidote to coercion is trust, not permissiveness.

If what you want from a child is truly non-negotiable, make that clear instead of pretending that it's a request until they say "no."

Children

We want to encourage generosity in our children rather than compliance.

Offer empathy to a child during a conflict only if you can imagine shifting your own position rather than as a subtle attempt to get them to change their mind.

Children

When we raise children with the trust that their needs matter as much as adults' needs, there is simply no reason for them to submit or rebel – there is nothing to rebel against!

Compliance will never contribute to a new
generation of people able to respond
empathically, to act in line with their deepest
values, or to take a courageous stand despite fear
of consequences.

Children

You cannot give children choice or take it away from them. Like everyone else, they always have it. The only power you have is to limit their options or their access to resources, and to deliver consequences to their choices that you don't like.

Raising children to believe that natural consequences and enforced consequences are equivalent diminishes their capacity to understand how the world works and to discern choice and its actual consequences.

Children

If we want to increase the chances of caring actions, I have no remaining doubt that the most effective method we can employ is to raise children without fear, so they can find and cultivate their own empathic sensibilities.

Choic

We are our c
- Jean-Paul

We choose neither the circumstances of our lives nor the consequences to our actions; we only have full choice about how we act within those constraints.

The more strategies, the more options.
The more options, the more choice.
The more choice, the less likely we are to
resort to violence.

Choice

It is sometimes easier to remember choice in extreme situations than in everyday life.

Saying things "nicely" is not the same as making room for the other person to have free choice and being open to hearing "no."

Choice

Justifying your choices is a way to pretend you haven't made them.

Moving toward full choice includes being able to receive another's request, however it is couched, in a way that maintains our own dignity, autonomy, and care.

Choice

Choice is at the heart of a radical consciousness
that can see and understand without reacting,
a consciousness that can stand up to authority
without losing love.

We can only choose "yes" when we can choose "no."

Choice

Choice is soft, empowered, intrinsic. If we are
tense, we are probably still reacting.

When I make a proactive choice about what
I want to do and make that my habit, I'm
more able to follow through more of
the time.

Choice

The significance of making a choice increases the less we like the options or the consequences. Making a choice is not about having no consequences – it's about overcoming the fear of consequences.

The more conscious we are of our needs,
the more freedom we have in finding
strategies that will truly meet those needs.

Choice

Our human need for autonomy is met through an internal process of conscious choice; it is not something others can meet for us.

If people cannot say "no" without incurring consequences, then they're not free. Then whatever they do for us is not a free gift. And if it's not a free gift, then sooner or later we pay for it – usually in the goodwill of the relationship.

Choice

When you are truly able to open your heart widely enough to hold all of the needs – those you are trying to meet, those that are met, those that are not met – then magic can happen. Each one of these needs is a vibrant, pulsating part of your heart and your humanity; each of them is your own life trying to happen. Honoring all of them breaks through your internal either/or, and can bring you to a place of true choice.

Collaboration

Individually, we are one drop.
Together, we are an ocean.
   – Ryunosuke Satoro

The more needs of more people included
in a solution, the more robust the solution.

More often than not, the path to the solution
that works for everyone starts with letting go of
focusing on the solution and instead shifting
awareness to how to maintain the connection in
the face of difference, disagreement,
or struggle.

Collaboration

If I really understand the needs of another person,
we have more options together.

If we can see conflict as an opportunity to
get to know ourselves and others better, we
improve our capacity to collaborate.

If enough people in power have enough moments
of seeing that well-crafted, well-facilitated
collaborative processes yield better results for all,
I retain the belief that over time the tide will shift.

Collaboration

True collaboration requires both love and courage, speaking and listening, and changing our habitual ways of acting to see and show more of what's really going on.

Communication

Eloquence is the power to translate a truth into language perfectly intelligible to the person to whom you speak.
– Ralph Waldo Emerson

I want my speech to be purpose-driven and
not rule-driven.

The real work of making communication work is internal; it's working with the thought structures that separate us from other people even while we are trying to connect with them.

Communication

Any of us are more likely to speak when we feel able to express the truth and have a modicum of trust that we'll be heard.

We tend to hear what other people say through the lens of the effect that it has on us, rather than through understanding the meaning their actions have for them. If we can pay close attention to where comments are coming from, they might have a different effect on us.

Communication

I aim to maximize the ratio of meaning to the number of words.

Compassion

*If you want others to
be happy, practice
compassion.
If you want
to be happy,
practice compassion.*

– His Holiness the Dalai Lama

Compassion is often seen as an obstacle to decisive action to honor our own needs. I see compassion instead as an insurance policy of sorts. With compassion, my actions are motivated by care for everyone's needs. This allows me to trust that my action on behalf of my own needs will not be harmful to others because I hold them with care.

The "tragic" lens allows us to hold compassion for our human fallibility instead of wishing for perfection and judging everything else.

Compassion

Even when we find someone's action loathsome, it is still motivated by some needs similar to our own. If we can uncouple that person's action from the need, we can easily wish for them to have that need met. This allows us to shift from mistrust and judgment to a sense of tragedy that we can hold with compassion.

Cultivating needs awareness is one clear
path to growing the muscle of compassion.

Compassion

We are habituated to create a dichotomy
between compassion and responsibility.
Truly compassionate solutions to conflict arise
from finding non-punitive ways to attend
to responsibility.

Courage

Life shrinks or expands in proportion to one's courage.

– Anais Nin

It is so difficult to swim against the tide of the way things are. It is precious that some of us have the courage to do so.

Overcoming our fear of being intrusive requires us to accept the power of our love and care and existence as a gift, including the discomfort it might bring to another person.

Courage

Part of my definition of courage is not
only facing up to potential consequences
but also keeping my heart open, loving,
and unprotected while doing it.

Time and again, I have come back to the
same clarity: when I judge, I am protected
in some way. I don't have to feel whatever is
going on in its fullness.

Courage

When people have done significant harm, it takes enormous courage to traverse the sea of shame that separates them from their own weeping soul.

Speaking of love alone is not enough to prevent violence. In addition, we need the courage to face consequences, whether physical or emotional, so we can love fearlessly and remain soft and open enough to respond nonviolently to what we don't like.

Courage

The more we are willing to stand up and ask questions at all times, the more likely we are to maintain our moral courage in extreme circumstances.

It takes courage to move closer to the edges of our confidence, so that more and more of us choose to bring forth our gifts and vulnerabilities – qualities needed for the immense task of making the world work for all of us.

Courage

There is a kind of courage that I treasure:
being ready to look at what is happening with an
openness to being touched, affected, moved, and
possibly changed in the process. It comes hand in
hand with care in action, including the willingness
to pay a personal cost and to give up comfort and
convenience in standing up for the things we
care about.

Courage is fueled by the conviction of truth and integrity, coupled with the abiding trust in love's power. The intensity of love and commitment serves as a form of fire that burns through perceived danger. This kind of love is not dependent on the behavior of others.
This love continues even in the extreme of enduring violence against self when engaging in nonviolent resistance.

Courage

Complete courage is about building the willingness to lose everything and still be at peace with it.

Dialogue

In true dialogue, both sides are willing to change.

– Thich Nhat Hanh

True dialogue can only happen if I enter the conversation willing to be changed by it. If I am unwilling to change, to be affected sufficiently to consider options new to me, on what grounds am I expecting the other person to change?

Dialogue is the most collaborative when we
frame questions that don't compromise our
own power or the dignity of the other.

Dialogue

The goal of dialogue is to see whether we can close the gap between our own perceptions and preferred strategies and those of another person.

I continue to work on being able to say "no" without closing my heart in defiance, and on being able to say "yes" with full generosity and willingness, even when someone is in a position of authority and I perceive there is no room for dialogue.

Dialogue

Ending everything we say with a question
keeps the dialogue going because it invites
a response.

The discipline of dialogue, at its heart, is a commitment to continue pursuing an outcome that truly works for everyone — even when others are only looking out for their own interest.

Dialogue

If there's a right answer to a question, it's
going to feel like a demand.

Empathy

If we could read the secret history of our enemies, we should find in each man's life sorrow and suffering enough to disarm all hostility.

– Henry Wadsworth Longfellow

I don't want to secretly punish people who believe in punishment. I want to grasp what their needs are and support them even if I don't support their strategy.

When I am in empathy, it's as if I am the
other person while knowing clearly that
I am not.

Empathy

Empathy is not a commodity or a resource that I give. It's a magical space I enter into.

When people are heard well, they are more
able to hear others.

Empathy

Agreement does not easily lead to empathy.
Agreement keeps us at the level of content.
Empathy arises at a different level of
meaning, closer to the core of our shared
human experience of responding to life
moment by moment.

The more challenging it is to viscerally step into the experience of another, the more necessary it is to do so in order to mend the separation. Whatever else is true, what is foreign to me, what is challenging, what is frightening, what I may judge, are also part of life. By distancing myself from these, I remain closed to some aspect of life.

Empathy

When we are in pain about someone else's action, cultivating compassion for and understanding of the needs that led to their actions can be a source of relief from the pain.

Empathy integrates mind and heart in
the very same act of bringing together
self and other.

Empathy

Behind every complaint there's a vision.

Other people's actions and thoughts make as
much sense to them as ours do to us.

True empathy requires a degree of risk taking, openness, and vulnerability, as our offering of empathy may not be received as a gift.

Empathy

Empathic presence with another is also a gift
to ourselves: the gift of being nourished by the
trust of another, by witnessing pure, distilled,
raw humanity in its unmistakable beauty.

Freedom

For to be free is not merely to cast off one's chains, but to live in a way that respects and enhances the freedom of others.

– Nelson Mandela

Inner freedom is my own ability to choose
from inside how I respond to what life puts
on my path. No one can take that away
from me.

We cannot go all the way to freedom
without crying.

Freedom

Being conscious of my needs, finding acceptance
for them, and embracing the discomfort of being
with my feelings form the foundation that gives
me more freedom to respond to life.

Freedom, for me, resides in the dialogic stance,
"I would like to (fill in the blank) and I truly want
to know whether or not that works for you."

Freedom

When we engage fully with uncertainty, the
unknown, and the impossibility of control,
then we move toward liberation.

Rebellion is not true freedom, because we are reacting to the terms set by another rather than simply pursuing the path we want to pursue.

Freedom

Our true freedom is rooted in coming back, again and again, to the needs we are trying to meet, and then making choices that appear most likely to meet them, without ever knowing if they will.

True inner freedom is closer to the original meaning of autonomy – living by one's own laws. There is nothing reactive, defiant, resistant, or defensive about it. Instead, it comes calmly and softly from within, giving us more resilience when engaging with others.

Freedom

When I react to not having my needs met by
closing down and not wanting, then I imprison
myself. To the extent that I can allow myself
to keep wanting that which I cannot have,
I have more freedom as a human being.

Grief

The most beautiful people we have known are those who have known defeat, known suffering, known struggle, known loss, and have found their way out of the depths. These persons have an appreciation, a sensitivity, and an understanding of life that fills them with compassion, gentleness, and a deep loving concern. Beautiful people do not just happen.

– Elisabeth Kübler-Ross

Any grieving we don't do stiffens our hearts
and shuts us away from fully engaging
with life.

Grieving – letting myself cry and cry and rip my heart open without blaming, without grasping for change, and without contracting – frees up enough energy to keep my heart open.

Grief

Grieving the past enables me to be stronger
to face the present.

When people have blood on their hands, they
need enough love to find their way back into
their own heart to grieve all they have done
and maintain some hope of belonging, again,
in the community of humans.

Grief

We cannot change what happened in the past, nor the fact that it may well continue to happen again and again. But if we find acceptance, we can have more choice about how to meet life.

Unless we allow ourselves to connect with
the dream that lives in us, and experience
all the grief that comes from seeing the gap
between the dream and the reality around
us, we are going to stay in the reality that is
not the dream.

Grief

Bliss means having no resistance to the flow
of life through me, whatever form it takes.

Healing

As my suffering mounted, I soon realized that there were two ways in which I could respond to my situation – either to react with bitterness or seek to transform the suffering into a creative force. I decided to follow the latter course.

– Martin Luther King Jr.

It can be harder to heal from having harmed
others than from harm done to us.

Sometimes I only know that I have healed
from something when I experience gratitude
for it having happened.

Healing

When we have been harmed, one of the biggest obstacles to healing is distrusting everyone's humanity.

When we can show someone a possible way to make sense of another person's apparently inhuman acts, the relief and restoration of possibility are almost indescribable. Something melts that may have been encrusted for decades. For a moment, or forever, there is an opening back into the fullness of life.

Healing

Restoring our lost connection to our soul requires us to face tremendous shame, and it's only love that can support us in doing so.

Integrity

I am not bound to win,
but I am bound to be true.
I am not bound to succeed,
but I am bound to live up
to what light I have.

– Abraham Lincoln

Nonviolence means the willingness to keep showing up and behaving in the world in integrity with who I want to be regardless of how others act.

If I want to build a future world beyond punishment and reward, I will aim to live this future in the present in every moment with every person in every interaction.

Integrity

We cannot have complete integrity without cultivating the courage to face potential consequences that might come our way when we act in line with our values.

I want to find, accept, and then stretch my limits so I can take bolder and bolder actions in the face of fear.

There will always be people who see the implementation of our vision as an absolute threat to what they hold most dear. And we will need to include and embrace their needs and well-being in full if we are to operate with integrity.

Integrity

Whether or not I create what I want in the world, I want to die knowing that I lived with the integrity of trying.

Interdependence

We can either emphasize those aspects of our traditions, religious or secular, that speak of hatred, exclusion, and suspicion or work with those that stress the interdependence and equality of all human beings. The choice is yours.

– Karen Armstrong

In a separated world, I can attend to my needs
or to your needs, not to both. In a chosen
interdependent world, I can embrace both.

The vision of a world where everyone's needs matter appeals to people intuitively. Nonetheless, the capacity to hold our own and others' needs at the same time remains beyond reach in the face of apparent scarcity that pits us against each other.

Interdependence

People come fully alive when they tell or hear stories of giving to others. Yet we continue to proclaim an illusory self-sufficiency in which we don't ask for what we need. Interdependence requires a shift from the illusion of self-sufficiency to the freedom that comes when we can accept our dependence on others for the fulfillment of our needs.

Interdependence requires distinguishing between independence as the human capacity for free choice of action, and the choice to act without consideration of others' needs.

Interdependence

As we grow in our capacity for interdependence,
we learn to recognize that asking for support
provides an opportunity for others to contribute.

Interdependence relies on holding everyone's needs with care, including my own, and transcending the either/or of "selfishness" vs. "selflessness."

Interdependence

We absolutely need others to help us sort the maze of our relationships, both within ourselves and with others. We carry shame about needing support, as if such need is a problem rather than a basic expression of our interdependent nature as human beings.

Leadership

*I never did anything alone.
Whatever was accomplished in
this country was accomplished
collectively.*

- Golda Meir

However challenging, transforming the legacy of domination to collaborative leadership is essential to our survival.

If you don't enjoy what a leader is doing, then, instead of criticizing the leader, step in as the leader's ally and intervene in a way that holds everyone with care and dignity.

Leadership

Transformation and empowerment are enhanced when we can allow our leaders to make mistakes and we remain open to being inspired and moved by their vision and actions.

The more I can remember the disempowerment
and isolation that filters how people hear me,
the more I might succeed in expressing myself in
ways that allow people to awaken directly to our
interdependence.

Leadership

If you are not a designated leader,
you nonetheless hold a key power:
the power of your heart and mind to listen,
to love, to create connection, and to
empower people.

I want to balance between leaving people alone as they struggle to find an answer and giving it to them, the latter of which will not help them find it tomorrow.
I hold faith that people can find their own answers. I strive to see that my role is to ask just enough leading questions to help them along their path to self-discovery.

Leadership

One key obstacle to collaborative leadership is the tragic phenomenon of pervasive disempowerment, which makes the challenge of collaborating from above that much more difficult. People hear demands when they are asked to do something by a leader; they remain cynical about efforts to solicit their input and participation in decision-making; or they persist in not expressing themselves honestly even when a leader is committed to creating a no-reprisal environment.

I'd like to believe that we can use our small-scale efforts at non-cooperation with the status quo, at the creation of alternatives, and at consciousness transformation to get us all ready, so that when the window opens up, we will be available to respond to the call: to offer inspiration and clarity that can make a decisive difference.

Leadership

Embodying collaborative leadership requires us to become ever more aware of the potential abuses of power that stem from our own and others' habits.

Collaborating for change points to a vision of leaders as stewards of the whole. Even when people are opposed to our proposed changes, this understanding enables us to maintain a commitment to include their needs in the mix of what we are trying to create.

Leadership

You don't have to overcome all your
limitations in order to step into leadership.

Love

Your task is not to seek for love, but merely to seek and find all the barriers within yourself that you have built against it.

– Rumi

Human souls are irresistible. When we truly see another human soul, we can't help but fall in love.

All the love and understanding in the world
is not a substitute for action that brings
concrete and material results. The point of
love is to ensure that our actions are free
of violence, hatred, and separation.

Love

The networks of love in which we are embedded are both tenuous and strong, like fine spider silk with its tensile strength greater than steel.

Love implies envisioning, engaging in dialogue, and even organizing nonviolent resistance in order to create a world that truly works for everyone, even our former enemies.

Love

Empathy is one of our most reliable ways to express love. It's precisely those people who are capable of active cruelty, those that are hardest for us to love, that are most in need of it.

Mattering

*I've learned that people will forget
what you said, people will forget what
you did, but people will never forget
how you made them feel.*

– Maya Angelou

What we have to offer, who we are, matters. The world would be different if we were not here.

We all know how to let people know they matter. In this way, at whatever scale we operate, we can model the world we want to create.

Mattering

Knowing that we matter is the glue and
lubricant of all human interaction.

People who don't know they matter are more
likely to cause harm than those who have a
clear sense of their place in the human family.

To know that I matter is both a huge
relief and a huge responsibility.

Mattering

There is an epidemic of people who think they have nothing to offer. The vaccine for this societal illness is for all of us to ask ourselves and others to take ourselves seriously. So, please, take away the "I don't know," ignore the voices that tell you that you don't know or that you don't matter, and speak what is inside you. That will be evidence that you matter...and that you are part of the cure.

People are often more likely to leave a group believing they don't "fit in" rather than to recognize that they are, by definition, an integral part of the group. By choosing active participation, you help shape the group's nature and actions

Mattering

When we trust that our needs matter, we are much more flexible about how they are going to be met. We are even more flexible about whether they will be met at all.

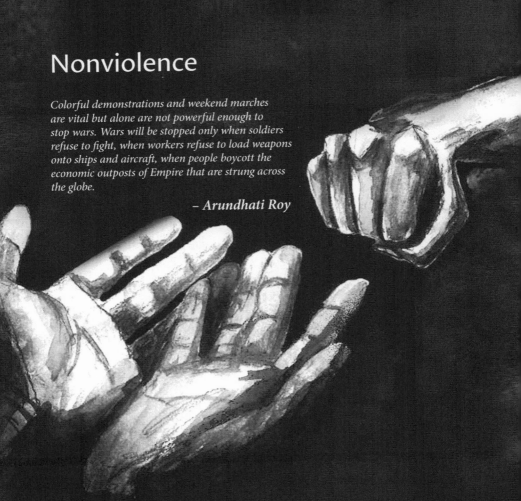

Nonviolence

Colorful demonstrations and weekend marches are vital but alone are not powerful enough to stop wars. Wars will be stopped only when soldiers refuse to fight, when workers refuse to load weapons onto ships and aircraft, when people boycott the economic outposts of Empire that are strung across the globe.

– Arundhati Roy

Nonviolence is a chosen, mindful approach
to life that emerges from standing for love,
courage, and truth.

Nonviolent resistance, as I understand it,
is about standing up with love to those with
power who are not ready to dialogue, who are
committed to their own power despite our
most well-intentioned efforts to engage
with them, who contribute, by their very
business-as-usual daily decisions, to
ongoing massive destruction.

Nonviolence

Being able to accept repression while standing for a vision of a different world often requires much more courage than fighting back.

If I am operating as an ambassador for a new consciousness, I do the work. I use language that makes sense to others who are not part of my community of commitment, so that they don't have to work harder to hear and understand me.

Nonviolence

The passage into nonviolence is doubly courageous: it requires the courage to overcome internal reactive habits, and the courage to face the potential consequences that arise from standing up to those in power, especially when they are fully committed to subjugating resisters.

The only thing that interferes with complete
nonviolence is fear.

Nonviolence

Fear itself doesn't go away as the practice of nonviolence deepens. What changes is the ability to bear it and still choose love and courage. With enough practice and commitment, fear-based action becomes less and less attractive.

The only way I can imagine to reach a livable
future for all is based on nonviolent means.

Nonviolence

Whatever else is true, I am confident that the more we can all learn to integrate the options of dialogue and nonviolent resistance into our body, mind, and soul, the less likely it is that we would resort to killing as the only option in any given circumstance.

Nonviolence obtains its power from love, from breaking down the barriers of separation and cultivating compassion for everyone, from the courage to face consequences to our actions, from the willingness to stand for truth, and from the fierce commitment to overcome fear and act in integrity.

Nonviolence

Nonviolence is about finding the courage and love to bring truth at times when our values are being violated, interfering with our own or others' human needs. It's the willingness to stand up for what's of value to us while remaining openhearted toward those who see things differently.

Power

*The most common way people give up
their power is by thinking they don't
have any.*

– Alice Walker

Power is simply the capacity to mobilize resources to attend to needs. We all need power.

Part of becoming powerful rests on the capacity
to hold the thread of intention up against the
juiciness of the present moment.

Power

Transcending the paradigm of submission
and rebellion means asking for what we want
without giving away our own power and
without taking away the power of others.

One of the resources that people in power
draw on is other people's reluctance to
say "no."

Whenever people "buy" their needs through fear-and-reward-based compliance, they are bound to know, somewhere deep within, that they are outside the web of interdependence and love.

Power

I don't know how we will reach the people in power. I only know that the task is essential if we are to survive these times and emerge as a species that thrives within the web of life on this planet.

I have seen people defer to me when I didn't ask them to do so. I have felt the pain of separation and loneliness when people give away their power. I have also seen people respond to me in defiance and rebellion, reacting to what I didn't say or do just because I am in power.

Power

If you have access to your sense of power,
you are unlikely to feel angry.

Practice

There is no such thing as a difficult [musical] piece. A piece is either impossible or it is easy. The process whereby it migrates from one category to the other is known as practicing.

– Louis Kentner

The only thing I know for sure about human nature is that we are creatures of practice: we become what we do.

My favorite form of practice is to take small steps that model the way I want to be and gradually result in new habits. Small steps taken consistently go far.

Practice

Practice is a training of the mind, heart, and body that provides the scaffolding for change to take place in a gentle and self-loving way.

Practice needs to be doable so we don't
get discouraged.

Practice reduces the gap between what we
long for and what we can embody.

Practice

Understanding the consciousness of nonviolence
– even embracing it, choosing it, loving it,
believing in it wholeheartedly – is not sufficient
because the old ways are so embedded in us,
and we in them. This is why we need practice.

Presence

The capacity to give one's attention to a sufferer is a very rare and difficult thing; it is almost a miracle; it is a miracle. Nearly all those who think they have the capacity do not possess it.

— *Simone Weil*

Presence is wordless. It's about making our
being available to be with another person's
experience instead of being focused on
our own.

I want to cultivate complete presence with the intensity of feelings so that I can stay grounded in more and more circumstances and situations.

Presence

The emotional charge – of anger, fear, shame, or belief in our own inadequacy or in other people's bad intentions – is the surest way to rob us of what capacity we have, rendering us incapable of expressing ourselves without blaming the other and of maintaining curious, empathic presence.

I want to do all I can, in the presence of
suffering of any kind, to let people know
I am with them, that they are not holding
their pain alone. I trust that this is the
most significant gift I can offer – my own
full heart and presence.

Presence

The greatest effect I can have on the world is to be 100 percent present when I am with someone. If I'm thinking about what I could do somewhere else, with someone else, or in some other way, I'm not present, and I have less ability to have an effect now.

Relationships

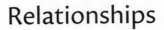

Piglet sidled up to Pooh from behind.
"Pooh!" he whispered. "Yes, Piglet?"
"Nothing," said Piglet, taking Pooh's
paw. "I just wanted to be sure of you."

– *A.A. Milne*

One source of difficulty in relationships comes from seeing honesty and care as mutually exclusive, instead of recognizing the extraordinary possibilities that arise when we bring our dilemmas, our sorrows and doubts, and our less-than-together selves to each other at the same time that we bring our love, empathy, and understanding.

As soon as any difference arises between what we want and what someone else wants, our habits direct us to push or give up. The alternative is to aim for solutions that work for both of us.

Relationships

When we can truly hold together both of our needs, we either find a solution that works for both of us or together we grieve its absence without losing connection.

Resentment comes from doing things I am
not truly willing to do, not from any actions
of my partner.

Relationships

If our connection depends on hiding my
authentic self, the relationship is neither a
true nor a sustainable connection.

Severing the ties of a relationship with someone without learning how to assert our needs, is more likely to land us in new relationships that recreate the same patterns.

Relationships

As a couple, you can shift from having a conflict to exploring a dilemma for which you have shared responsibility.

Transforming a relationship includes
releasing all the invisible contracts, so that we
do only what we can do willingly and without
secretly expecting something in return.

Relationships

Taking 100 percent responsibility for a relationship means that I do all in my power to ensure that I and my partner attend to our own needs and each other's.

Resilience

*You can't stop the waves,
but you can learn to surf.*

– Jon Kabat-Zinn

Fundamentally, we all live in a society where human needs are more often not met than met, especially in our early years. That makes most of us very non-resilient, in that having an experience of unmet needs can be very distressing for us. We all bring this lack of resilience with us to all our relationships, which makes it harder to navigate differences in strategies, an essential feature of conflict.

I become stronger and more resilient the more
I can shed the layers of protection that separate
me from asking for what I need.

We can increase our resilience by
embracing a consistent spiritual practice that
strengthens our ability to withstand unmet needs,
so that we can access choice in how to respond
to those difficult moments.

Resilience

Vision in itself can be a source of energy
and resilience, as it rekindles our passion
to find more capacity to accept obstacles
along the way.

Self-Acceptance

Friendship with oneself is all important,
because without it one cannot be friends
with anyone else in the world.

– Eleanor Roosevelt

I want to increase my capacity to close the
gap between my actions and my values with
self-acceptance. The basic premise is simple:
any action that I take, no matter how much
it aligns with my values, is an attempt to
meet some basic human needs. If I can
identify and connect with those needs,
I increase my self-acceptance.

With self-acceptance comes the possibility
of learning and growth, which don't
tend to happen within the context of
self-judgment.

I am not afraid of my judgments. I want to
engage with them long enough to get the
information that I need to connect with
my heart.

Self-Acceptance

If you can accept your reactivity, then you'll be less exhausted by it and more capable of gradually transcending it rather than suppressing it.

Trust

The heart can see beyond our prayers,
Beyond our fondest dreams
And tell us which are made for fools
And which are wise men's dreams.
Trust your heart.
Trust your heart.

– Judy Collins

Trust is to a collaboration-based social order what fear is to an authority-based social order. Trust, then, is the glue that binds everyone together in a large-scale society or organization.

When I trust myself, I am empowered to
stop looking to others for my safety.

Trust

Trust is not requiring reality to be a certain way.

While trying to build trust, ask only those questions whose answers you will believe.

The paradox of trust: if I don't trust someone, more often than not they probably don't trust me either.

Trust

When we repair lost trust, there is less
anxiety about losing it again, because
we know we can recover it again.

Vulnerability

*Embracing our vulnerabilities is risky
but not nearly as dangerous as giving
up on love and belonging and joy –
the experiences that make us the most
vulnerable. Only when we are brave
enough to explore the darkness will we
discover the infinite power of the light.*

– Brené Brown

The path of vulnerability invites us to accept risks, stretch our wings, and recognize our resilience and capacity to survive that which we fear.

One tool that helps me gather up the courage to be vulnerable is finding my own inner acceptance, which can then nourish and protect me if others don't.

Vulnerability

The move toward violence emerges from
intense shame, from the difficulty in
resting in our vulnerability.

The risks of social isolation, humiliation, and loss of respect are as frightening to the emotional self as is physical danger. Although our emotional self might be "injured" or "die" as we open ourselves to truth and love in our interactions with ourselves and other humans, the practice of vulnerability invites us to do just that: take that risk and remain open.

Vulnerability

When I appreciate and accept the
opportunity to be open, raw, and so
fully human, I notice a shift in my energy and
acutely feel the freshness of life.

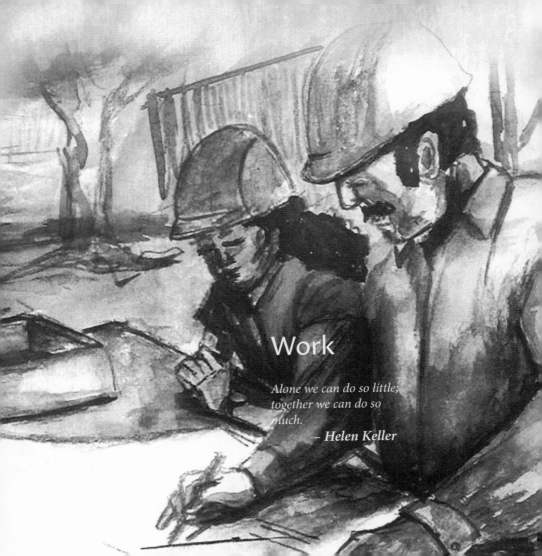

Work

*Alone we can do so little;
together we can do so
much.*

— *Helen Keller*

Explaining why we want something done
increases people's willingness to do it.

Efficiency is possible without compromising collaboration and empowerment. It requires empowering, effective, and transparent leadership.

Work

Helping others be conscious of their needs enables them to access personal resources to solve their problems on their own.

If you focus on what's possible in each situation rather than on what's fair, you will solve more problems faster.

Without hearing the truth about the human cost of any action, leaders lack critical feedback for making informed choices. Agreements based on fear of consequences are less authentic and less likely to last. When people don't feel free to say "no," they are less likely to give of themselves fully and take ownership of the work they do.

Work

When we see means and ends as one,
we can live every moment, personally
and as leaders, in courageous pursuit
of love and truth.

Author

ABOUT THE AUTHOR

Miki Kashtan is an internationally renowned and widely published authority on the practical applications of nonviolence in everyday life, basing her work primarily on Nonviolent Communication (NVC). She is a co-founder of Bay Area Nonviolent Communication (www.baynvc.org) in Oakland, CA, and a certified trainer with the international Center for Nonviolent Communication (www.cnvc.org). She has used her skills as a trainer, speaker, organizational consultant, meeting facilitator, and coach working on multiple continents.

Her writing has appeared in Psychology Today, Tikkun, Waging Nonviolence, Shareable, and her own blog, The Fearless Heart. She is the author of *Spinning Threads of Radical Aliveness: Transcending the Legacy of Separation in Our Individual Lives.* She holds a Ph.D. in sociology from the University of California at Berkeley.

WHERE TO READ MORE
BY MIKI KASHTAN

Miki Kashtan has written more than 220 posts on her blog,
The Fearless Heart. She generally posts weekly, and conducts
teleseminars to discuss her posts with all comers. These are
deeply thoughtful pieces that have delved into or touched
upon most of the topics in *The Little Book of Courageous Living*.
At The Fearless Heart (thefearlessheart.org) you can also
find links to her online published articles and news about
her upcoming books.

TRAININGS AND
ORGANIZATIONAL SERVICES

Follow links on The Fearless Heart site to the workshops, retreats, and teleseminars that Miki offers, in the Bay Area, on the phone, across the U.S., and in other countries. She and her colleagues at BayNVC also offer services to organizations to assist them in developing a culture of collaboration and in aligning their policies, practices, and procedures with their stated values. In addition, she has developed Convergent Facilitation, a decision-making process based on Nonviolent Communication that allows groups to reach a collaborative decision with fluency and grace and without creating polarization, animosity, or resentment. More information about such services, including contact information, can be found at thefearlessheart.org.

Made in the USA
San Bernardino, CA
17 May 2014